Positive Vibes
An Adult Coloring Book

ColoKara

Copyright © 2018 ColoKara

All rights reserved.

No part of this publication may be copied, reproduced in any format, by any means, electronic or otherwise, without prior consent from the copyright owner and publisher of this book.

Shutterstock Authors: Credit to - Julia Snegireva, Alicedaniel, Natsa, Katika, ImHope, Soffi Sk, Photo-nuke, Cerama_ama, Toporovska Nataliia, Lexver, Helen Lane, OlichO, Argunika, Ilonitta, Emila, Solyannikova, Sablegear, Palomita, NadiiaZ, Alfmaler

Here's a special gift from ColoKara for purchasing this coloring book!

You can now freely download these coloring pages at any time and print them out as many times as you want!

Get your FREE coloring pages from this link: https://colokara.com/positive-vibes-green

HAPPY COLORING!

Made in the USA
Las Vegas, NV
03 January 2023